HANDLING THE SHIFT TO T+1 IN THE FINANCIAL SECTOR

Comprehending the Shift, Consequences, and Prospects of Financial Market Settlements

Steve k. Bryant

Copyright

Copyright © 2024 by Steve k. Bryant

All rights reserved. No part of this publication may be reproduced, distributed, or transmitted in any form or by any means, including photocopying, recording, or other electronic or mechanical methods, without the prior written permission of the publisher, except in the case of brief quotations embodied in critical reviews and certain other noncommercial uses

Contents

Introduction of T+1 8
    An Overview of the Significance of the Shortened Settlement Cycle 8
    Importance of T+1 9
    Subheading to note Effect on Entities in the Market: 13
    Note Important Distinctions Between Transitions from T+3 to T+2 and T+2 to T+1 13

Chapter 1 15
The World's Transition to T+1 15
    The Journey of the US, Canada, and Mexico 15
    The US's Road to T+1 16
    Effect on the United States Market: 18
    The Trip to T+1 from Canada 20
    The Trip from Mexico to T+1 22

Chapter 2: 27
The United Kingdom Approves T+1 27
    Policies and Government Approval Requirements ... 27
    Policies and Government Approval Requirements ... 27
    Imperatives for Policy: 28
    Context and the Process of Making Decisions 29
    First Conversations and Viability Research 29

Establishment of the Task Force for Accelerated Settlement 30
Engagement with Stakeholders and Consultation 30
Policy Decisions and Official Approval 31
Compliance with the Transition in North America ... 32
Technological Readiness 32
Adjustments for operations 33
Market Effect and Benefits to Clients 33
Obstacles and Countermeasures 33
Prospects for the Future 34

Chapter 3 35
Getting Ready for the T+1 Rollout 35
The AST Report and Suggestions 35
A synopsis of the ten main suggestions 36
Priorities: Deadlines, Communication Strategies, and Operational Changes 38
The role and responsibilities of the technical group .. 39

Chapter 4 43
T+1 and Securities Finance 43
Securities Finance Market Dynamics 44
The Alignment of T+0 Trading with T+1 44
The Adaptation Strategies of EquiLend and Their Client Readiness 46

Chapter 5 48
Implementing Projects and Orders 48
  Important Modifications to Operations 48
  Technological Upgrades and Process Modifications. 49
  Mandatory Modifications to Operations Commencing in 2025 51
  Case Studies of Pioneers in the Field 52
Chapter 6 56
Interaction and Arrangement 56
  Strategies for Cross-European Communication 57
  The Value of Coordinated Schedules and Exchanged Best Practices 60
Chapter 7 63
The Road to T+1 in Europe 63
  ESMA's Request for Proof 63
  Goals of the Evidence Request 63
  Market Responses and Their Consequences 64
  Comprehensive Cost-Benefit Analysis 65
  Advantages 66
  Potential for a Combined T+1 Transition Schedule .. 68
Chapter 8 70
Takeaways from Europe and the US 70
  Comparative Evaluation 70

- Variations in Strategies for Implementation 70
- The state of the market and participant readiness 71
- Comparabilities Among Implementation Techniques 72
- Important Takeaways and Worldwide Uses 73
- Regulatory Support and Clarity 73
- Collaboration and Involvement of Stakeholders 75
- Improvements in Risk Management 76

Chapter 9 77

Settlers Cycles' Future 77
- Forecasts and Patterns 77
- Development Past T+1 77
- The Path Ahead: Strategic Points to Remember 81

Chapter 10 84

T+1's Economic Consequences 84
- Effects on the World Economy 85
- Financial Gains 85
- Financial Difficulties 86
- Examining T+1's Impact on the US Economy in 2024 88
- Broader implications for the market 89

Chapter 11 92

The Role of Technology in T+1 92
- Technological Enablers 92

    The Significance of Fintech Innovations and Blockchain 93

Chapter 12 97

Responses and Adjustments from the Global Market ... 97

    Regional Reactions and Approaches 98

    North America: Taking the Lead 98

    Europe: Progressive Adjustment 99

    Asia-Pacific: Diverse Advancements 100

Chapter 13 103

Wrap-Up 103

    A Synopsis of the Transfer to T+1 103

    Concluding Remarks Regarding Settlement Cycles' Future 105

    Addenda 106

    Appendix B: T+1 Implementation Timeline 107

    The UK government establishes the Accelerated Settlement Task Force in December 2022 108

    Technical Group Members and Their Roles, Appendix C 108

Introduction of T+1

An Overview of the Significance of the Shortened Settlement Cycle

The settlement cycle is a key element in the finance industry that determines when deals in the securities market are completed. Settlement cycles have traditionally been longer, giving sufficient time for the administrative work necessary to transfer ownership of shares. But as financial markets get more complex and technology becomes more advanced, there is a strong movement to shorten these cycles in order to improve efficiency, lower risk, and keep up with the quick speed of contemporary trade.

The time frame between the trade date (T) and the settlement date—when the seller must deliver the security and the buyer must make payment—is known as the settlement cycle. Significant reductions in this cycle have occurred over the decades. One important step in modernizing financial markets was the switch from T+3 (three business days after the trade date) to T+2 (two business days after the trade date). With the move to T+1 (one business day following the trading date), the sector is about to take another giant step ahead.

Importance of T+1

Diminished Counterparty Risk: Reducing counterparty risk is one of the main reasons for cutting the settlement cycle to T+1. This risk results from the chance that one of the parties to the transaction could go into default before the settlement is finalized. Exposure to this risk is greatly reduced by shortening the period of time between trade and settlement.

Enhanced Market Efficiency: A reduced settlement cycle may result in a more efficient market. It increases market liquidity by enabling faster reinvested money. Investors stand to gain from this since it may result in higher returns and increased financial market dynamism overall.

Operational Risk Reduction: Because errors or disruptions in the settlement process are possible, the longer the settlement period, the higher the operational risk. T+1 increases the dependability of financial transactions by streamlining procedures and reducing the window for operational errors.

Alignment with Contemporary Trading Practices: A T+1 settlement cycle is more in line with the expectations and speed of contemporary trading practices in a time of widespread high-frequency trading and instantaneous transactions. It guarantees that the trade actions occurring in the front office stay up with the back office procedures.

Global Competitiveness: Financial markets must embrace best practices and technology innovations in order to stay competitive on a worldwide basis. The move to T+1 is a component of a larger plan to guarantee that markets lead the way in efficiency and innovation.

Comparative Study: Transitions from T+3 to T+2 versus T+2 to T+1

The US securities settlement process saw a major improvement in both its efficiency and risk profile in 2017 with the completion of the switch from T+3 to T+2. The infrastructure, methods, and procedures of market players had to undergo significant modifications as a result of this shift. But the transition from T+2 to T+1 is anticipated to be even more difficult and revolutionary.

Changeover to T+2 from T+3 Historical Context and Intentions: The T+3 settlement cycle has been in place since the mid-1990s. The move to T+2 was driven by the need to reduce systemic risk and improve operational effectiveness. Significant events, like the 2008 financial crisis, highlighted the vulnerabilities associated with longer settlement timeframes, leading to industry-wide and regulatory initiatives to shorten the cycle.

Implementation Difficulties: Brokers, clearing agencies, custodians, and regulatory organizations had to work closely together to coordinate the shift to T+2. To account for the shortened cycle, systems and procedures have to be completely redesigned. This involved making adjustments to operational operations, upgrading technological platforms, and making sure that new regulatory requirements were met.

Realized Benefits: There were a number of benefits to switching to T+2, including a decrease in counterparty risk, a reduction in margin needs, and an improvement in market liquidity. More harmonization with global markets—many of which had previously embraced T+2 settlement cycles—was also promoted by it.

T+1 Transition from T+2

Increased Complexity: Compared to the preceding transition, the move from T+2 to T+1 is more complicated. The trading, clearing, and settlement operations must be precisely synchronized because the settlement period is shorter, which reduces margin for error.

Significant technological and operational modifications are required in order to implement the T+1 transition. Market players need to make investments in more sophisticated systems capable of managing data and processing in real time. This includes better reconciliation systems, improved market participant communication protocols, and process automation.

Regulatory and Compliance Considerations: In order to facilitate the T+1 settlement cycle, regulatory frameworks must be modified. This entails modifying regulatory monitoring, adjusting reporting requirements, and making sure market players adhere to the new deadlines.

Worldwide Implications and Coordination: To guarantee smooth cross-border transactions, worldwide coordination is required when various markets consider or adopt T+1 settlement cycles. To prevent fragmentation, cooperation between international regulatory agencies and coordination of settlement methods are needed.

Testing and Market Readiness: A lot of testing and modeling of the new settlement cycle is needed to make sure the market is ready for T+1. This entails performing industry-wide rehearsals, stress testing systems under various conditions, and verifying that all market participants can function efficiently within the compressed timeframe.

Subheading to note Effect on Entities in the Market:

Brokers and dealers: To guarantee that trades are executed and settled within the new timeframe, they must modify their front- and back-office processes. This calls for transaction confirmation and settlement processes to be more effective.

Custodians and clearing agents: They are essential to the settlement process and need to make sure their systems can manage the higher volume and faster transaction rates.

Institutional Investors: They may need to modify their portfolio management procedures in order to adapt their trading strategies and operational operations to the new settlement cycle.

Note Important Distinctions Between Transitions from T+3 to T+2 and T+2 to T+1

Degree of Change: The settlement cycle was cut in half when the T+2 to T+1 transition occurred, and it was cut in half again when the T+3 to T+2 transition occurred. The latter is a more significant modification that calls for a thorough reorganization of current procedures and systems.

Market Impact: The switch to T+1 is anticipated to have an even bigger impact on market operations than the T+2 change did. This is because there is less buffer time available for resolving inconsistencies and near-instantaneous processing is required.

Technical Requirements: The T+1 transition necessitates state-of-the-art systems that can process data in real-time, whereas the T+2 transition only required updates to current technology. This incorporates machine learning, blockchain, and AI developments to automate and expedite settlement procedures.

Operational Modifications: T+2 necessitated significant but doable operational modifications to current technologies and procedures. But the move to T+1 calls for a paradigm change in the processing and settlement of trades, putting more of a focus on automation and real-time data sharing.

Risk management: While there is a decrease in risk associated with both transitions, the switch to T+1 provides a more noticeable one in terms of counterparty and operational risk. Because of the shorter cycle, there is less exposure for market players to operational failures or possible default.

The adoption of T+1 signifies a noteworthy advancement in the development of financial markets. It demonstrates the industry's dedication to raising productivity, lowering risk, and keeping up with the quick speed of contemporary trade. The financial industry must prioritize this shift despite the significant obstacles since it could have a positive impact on market stability, liquidity, and global competitiveness. Global markets will be moving toward T+1, and a successful implementation will depend heavily on the lessons learnt from past transitions and technological breakthroughs.

Chapter 1

The World's Transition to T+1

The Journey of the US, Canada, and Mexico

Settlement cycles have seen major changes in the global financial scene, especially with the shift to a T+1 (Trade date plus one day) settlement time. The voyage of the US, Canada, and Mexico toward T+1 is examined in this chapter, along with the schedule for implementation, market effects, and early difficulties encountered in conjunction with the resolutions put into place.

The US's Road to T+1

Timeline and Effects of Implementation

The switch to T+1 is evidence of the United States' commitment to leading the charge in efforts to modernize and streamline the financial systems. After the successful transition from T+3 to T+2 in 2017, the trip started in earnest in the middle of the 2010s. The earlier shift offered a basis on which the T+1 transition could be constructed.

Initial Scheduling (2018–2020):

1. Discussions regarding the viability and advantages of switching to T+1 were started by industry stakeholders, such as the Securities and Exchange Commission (SEC), the Depository Trust & Clearing Corporation (DTCC), and other financial sector associations.

2. To comprehend the operational and technological requirements, preliminary research and consultations were carried out.

Engaging Stakeholders (2021)

1. The first official interactions with clearing houses, custodians, brokers, and technology suppliers took place.

2. The SEC published a proposal detailing the possible structure for T+1 implementation for public discussion.

Regulatory Acceptance in 2022–2023

1. The SEC included industry input into the final version of the rulemaking process.

2. Timelines and comprehensive guidelines were released, laying the groundwork for required adherence.

Testing and System Upgrades for 2023–2024

1. Market participants upgraded their IT infrastructure significantly.

2. To guarantee preparedness, extensive testing phases were instituted, which included industry-wide rehearsals.

Launch (May 27, 2024, May 28)

1. With the completion of the official switch to T+1 settlement, US securities trading entered a new chapter.

2. To handle any teething problems, post-implementation monitoring and changes were carried out.

Effect on the United States Market:

Decreased Risk: By drastically cutting counterparty and systemic risk, the shortened settlement cycle improved market stability.

Enhanced Liquidity: Quicker reinvested funds would increase market liquidity and facilitate more effective capital allocation.

Operational Efficiency: Real-time processing and automation became widely adopted as a result of the shift, which simplified back-office processes.

First Difficulties and Solutions

There were difficulties associated with the switch to T+1. These comprised operational, technological, and regulatory obstacles that needed to be solved in concert.

Readiness for Technology

Challenge: The challenge is in guaranteeing that every market player possesses the requisite technology infrastructure to facilitate T+1.

Resolution: Trading and settlement systems have been upgraded with significant investments. Through its Project Ion project, which investigated the use of distributed ledger technology (DLT) to facilitate quicker settlement cycles, the DTCC, in particular, played a crucial role in facilitating these changes.

Modifications to Operations

Challenge: Changing operational operations to account for the shortened settlement period presents a challenge.

Resolution: In order to reduce manual interventions and increase automation, market participants re-engineered their procedures. To guarantee that personnel were competent in the new workflows, training programs were put in place.

Coordination of Regulations

Challenge: The challenge is in assuring compliance and harmonizing regulatory standards across several jurisdictions.

Resolution: To unify regulations and ensure a seamless transition, the SEC closely collaborated with other regulatory agencies, such as the Commodity Futures Trading Commission (CFTC) and foreign colleagues.

Market Communication

Challenge: The challenge is in ensuring that all parties communicate and coordinate effectively.

Resolution: Clear and consistent communication was maintained throughout the transition process with the aid of frequent industry forums, webinars, and updates from regulatory organizations.

The Trip to T+1 from Canada
Timeline and Effects of Implementation

The close integration of North American financial markets is reflected in the trajectory of Canada's shift to T+1, which was comparable to that of the US.

Initial Research (2018–2020)

The Investment Industry Regulatory Organization of Canada (IIROC) and the Canadian Securities Administrators (CSA) carried out preliminary feasibility studies.

Consultations with stakeholders were helpful in determining readiness and possible obstacles.

Regulatory Structure for 2021

Market players were asked to provide feedback through consultation papers released by the IIROC and the CSA.

Proposed were changes to the regulations to allow for the transition to T+1.

Preparing for Technology and Operations in 2022–2023

1. There were extensive testing periods and system upgrades.

2. Alignment of deadlines and procedures was secured by cooperative efforts with the US.

Phase of Implementation (2024)

1. On May 27–28, 2024, Canada synchronized its go-live date with the US.

2. After implementation, ongoing observation and adjustment were done.

Effect on the Market in Canada:

Enhanced Market Efficiency: Like in the US, the shorter cycle increased market liquidity and efficiency.

Risk Mitigation: Risk mitigation lowered settlement risk and strengthened the financial system's resilience.

Operational Improvements: Encouraged a broad use of cutting-edge technologies and enhanced workflows within operations.

First Difficulties and Solutions

Like the US, Canada suffered a number of difficulties with the switch to T+1.

Integration of Systems

Challenge: The challenge is in ensuring that improved systems are seamlessly integrated across different market participants.

Resolution: A seamless integration was made possible by cooperative efforts with technology suppliers and the application of industry-standard protocols.

Coordinating with Stakeholders

Challenge: The challenge is in coordinating the actions of various market players, especially smaller companies with constrained resources.

Resolution: To help smaller businesses modernize their systems and procedures, the CSA and IIROC offered resources and support.

Adherence to Regulations

Challenge: The challenge is in guaranteeing adherence to the latest regulatory mandates within the designated timeframes.

Resolution: Market participants were able to achieve compliance through the use of clear rules and a phased implementation strategy.

The Trip from Mexico to T+1
Timeline and Effects of Implementation

Despite being in line with North American efforts, Mexico's transition to T+1 experienced particular difficulties because of its distinct legislative framework and market structure.

First Schedule (2019–2020)

1. The ComisiónNacionalBancaria y de Valores (CNBV) and the Bolsa Mexicana de Valores (BMV) started investigating the viability of T+1.

2. There were stakeholder discussions and initial impact analyses.

Market and Regulatory Alignment for 2021–2022

1. The CNBV solicited input from market participants by interacting with them and publishing draft regulations.

2. To ensure regional uniformity, efforts were made to coincide with US and Canadian schedules.

Improvements to the System and Testing (2023)

1. Market participants made substantial improvements to their systems for trading and settlement.

2. Testing and simulations conducted across the industry guaranteed preparation for the change.

Execution (May 27, 28 of 2024)

1. Mexico completed the switch to T+1 by coordinating its go-live date with the US and Canada.

2. Monitoring and post-implementation assistance were given to handle any problems that might have arisen.

Effect on the Market in Mexico

Enhanced Market Competitiveness: The change made Mexico a more alluring location for foreign investment.

Risk Reduction: By cutting the settlement cycle short, counterparty risk was minimized and market stability was improved.

Operational Efficiency: Encouraged technological investments and process enhancements, increasing market efficiency overall.

First Difficulties and Solutions

On its path to T+1, Mexico had to overcome a number of particular difficulties.

Readiness of Infrastructure

Challenge: Being sure that the current market infrastructure could accommodate T+1 settlement is the challenge.

Resolution: With assistance from the CNBV and industry groups, large investments in infrastructure and technological upgrades were made.

Engagement of Market Participants

Challenge: The challenge is in organizing and educating a wide range of market players, such as smaller brokers and investors.

Resolution: To guarantee that every participant was suitably prepared, a plethora of training programs and resources were made available.

Harmonization of Regulations

Challenge: The challenge is in balancing local market demands with worldwide standards and regulatory obligations.

Resolution: Mexican regulations were brought into compliance with international best practices through cooperative efforts with foreign regulatory authorities.

Operational and Cultural Adjustments:

Challenge: Adapting cultural norms and market practices to the quicker settlement cycle presents a challenge.

Resolution: Market participants were assisted in adjusting to the new rules by ongoing education and information initiatives.

A major turning point in the development of the world's financial markets has been reached with the US, Canada, and Mexico moving closer to T+1 settlement. While each nation had its own set of difficulties, they all aimed to lower risk, increase market efficiency, and streamline operational procedures. The concerted efforts made in these North American marketplaces demonstrate how crucial cooperation and coordination are to bringing about such revolutionary shifts. Lessons learnt and advantages realized from the rollout of T+1 will act as a model for other markets contemplating similar changes, laying the groundwork for a more robust and effective global financial system.

Chapter 2:

The United Kingdom Approves T+1

Policies and Government Approval Requirements

The UK has a long history of being one of the major financial centers of the globe. toward light of this, the choice to switch to a T+1 settlement cycle is an important step toward preserving and improving this status. This chapter examines the background of the decision-making process, the government's approval procedure, the underlying policy imperatives, and EquiLend's observations into the preparedness and ramifications for the financial market.

Policies and Government Approval Requirements

The UK decided to switch to a T+1 settlement cycle due to a mix of industry demands, regulatory anticipation, and pressure from the worldwide competition. The approval of this shift by the UK government demonstrates a dedication to guaranteeing the stability, effectiveness, and conformity of the financial markets with global norms.

Regulatory Vision: The modernization of financial market infrastructure has been given top priority by the

UK government, which is represented by financial regulatory organizations including the Bank of England and the Financial Conduct Authority (FCA). The objective of this program is to mitigate settlement risk, optimize operational efficacy, and guarantee the continued appeal of the UK's financial markets to international investors.

Industry Demand: Industry participants are increasingly in agreement that a faster settlement cycle might have a number of positive effects, such as less counterparty risk and increased liquidity. Large financial institutions that handle significant transaction volumes and institutional investors have been very vociferous in their demand.

Global Competitive Pressures: The UK is under competitive pressure to adopt T+1 standards in order to stay ahead of other important markets including the US, Canada, and Mexico. Sustaining synchronized settlement cycles is essential to enabling cross-border transactions and guaranteeing the UK's continued prominence in the international financial sphere.

Imperatives for Policy:
Risk Reduction: By reducing the amount of time that transactions need to be settled, a T+1 settlement cycle

greatly lowers the risk of counterparty default. By doing this, the window of opportunity for counterparties to experience possible defaults is reduced.

Operational Efficiency: More effective systems and procedures are required for a shorter settlement cycle. In the banking sector as a whole, this drive toward automation and real-time processing may result in further operational gains.

Market Liquidity: This is still another important advantage. A T+1 cycle increases total market liquidity by making transaction proceeds available for reinvestment more quickly.

Investor Confidence: By showcasing a dedication to implementing best practices and upholding strict standards of efficiency and integrity in the market, T+1 implementation is likely to increase investor confidence.

Context and the Process of Making Decisions

A thorough and cooperative process involving numerous stakeholders, including regulatory organizations, industry associations, financial institutions, and technology providers, led to the decision to switch to T+1 settlement in the UK.

First Conversations and Viability Research

The effort started with preliminary talks about the viability and possible advantages of a T+1 settlement cycle amongst important parties. Feasibility studies by industry associations and consulting firms, which looked at the operational, technological, and legal ramifications of such a shift, provided support for these debates.

Establishment of the Task Force for Accelerated Settlement

1. The Accelerated Settlement Task Force was established by the UK government in December 2022 with the aim of formally investigating the feasibility of a quicker settlement cycle. The London Stock Exchange, the Bank of England, the FCA, and other trade associations were represented on the task force.

2. The task force was assigned the responsibility of carrying out an exhaustive evaluation of the settlement infrastructure as it currently exists, determining the modifications necessary to facilitate T+1, and creating an implementation schedule.

Engagement with Stakeholders and Consultation

1. Significant market participant participation and consultation were essential components of the decision-making process. Surveys, roundtable talks, and public consultation documents were used in order to get input and determine whether the market was prepared for the changeover.

2. Important issues brought up during the consultation process were the necessity of large-scale technology improvements, the possibility of upsetting current

processes, and the significance of coordinated global initiatives.

Leadership and Technical Group

1. Andrew Douglas was named chair of the Accelerated Settlement Task Force's Technical Group in April 2024. Douglas offered considerable knowledge to the role having worked in the post-trade space for over 35 years.

2. The Technical Group was in charge of laying out the specific procedures needed for the changeover, establishing timelines, and making sure that every market player was ready for the shift to T+1.

Policy Decisions and Official Approval

1. In early 2024, the UK government formally approved the transition to T+1 based on task force recommendations and consultations. A thorough implementation schedule and rules for market players backed the policy choice.

2. The UK's official T+1 implementation date was set for before December 31, 2027, while the Technical Group specified that operational modifications begin on a date in 2025.

EquiLend's Outlook and Readiness

Leading post-trade solutions provider in the securities finance space, EquiLend is ready for the UK to adopt T+1, having closely synchronized with the changeover in

North America. Head of post-trade solutions at EquiLend Gabi Mantle has been a strong proponent of the switch to T+1, stressing the company's preparedness as well as the wider implications for the sector.

Compliance with the Transition in North America

With its active participation in the US, Canada, and Mexico T+1 transition, EquiLend has laid a strong basis for its preparedness in the UK. The infrastructure and procedures of the company are already designed to accommodate quick settlement cycles, guaranteeing a seamless transition for its clients.

Technological Readiness

1. To enable T+1, EquiLend has made significant investments in modernizing its system. This entails improving its infrastructure for trading and settlement in order to enable automation, better data management, and real-time processing.

2. The company's products have features that speed up the transaction confirmation, settlement, and reconciliation processes in order to meet the rising demands of a shorter settlement cycle.

Adjustments for operations

1. EquiLend has made a number of operational improvements to guarantee smooth operations under T+1. This entails streamlining processes, cutting down on manual interventions, and improving counterparty and client communications.

2. In order to help them adjust to the new settlement cycle and make sure they are ready for the change, EquiLend has given its clients extensive training and resources.

Market Effect and Benefits to Clients

1. From EquiLend's point of view, the market and its customers should benefit greatly from the switch to T+1. These advantages include higher market liquidity, lower counterparty risk, and improved operational effectiveness.

2. The enhanced speed and dependability of transactions will benefit EquiLend's clientele, which includes significant financial institutions and asset managers. This will enable better risk management and more effective capital utilization.

Obstacles and Countermeasures

1. EquiLend recognizes that there are a number of obstacles associated with the shift to T+1, such as the requirement for significant system changes and possible disruptions to ongoing operations. To address these

issues, the company has implemented strong mitigating methods.

2. EquiLend maintains up-to-date knowledge of innovations and regulatory requirements through ongoing contact with industry associations and regulatory agencies. This enables timely modifications and compliance.

Prospects for the Future

1. EquiLend anticipates a more widespread global use of T+1 settlement cycles. The company is certain that the UK's successful implementation will serve as a model for other economies, resulting in additional efficiency and lower levels of risk in the world financial system.

2. EquiLend is dedicated to helping its customers during and after this change, always developing its products to satisfy the shifting demands of the industry.

The UK made a calculated decision to improve the effectiveness, stability, and international competitiveness of its financial markets by switching to a T+1 settlement cycle. The extensive and inclusive government approval process made sure that all interested parties were taken into account

and ready for the changeover. The readiness and viewpoint of EquiLend underscore the significance of technology innovation and operational expertise in effectively managing this momentous transition.

Lessons learnt and advantages realized will be useful benchmarks for other markets contemplating similar transitions as the UK pushes on with T+1 implementation. The concerted actions of industry associations, market players, and regulatory agencies highlight the shared commitment to creating a more robust and effective global financial system. The switch to T+1 is more than just a technical upgrade; it is a transformative step towards the future of financial markets, promising a safer, more efficient, and more dynamic trading environment.

Chapter 3

Getting Ready for the T+1 Rollout

The AST Report and Suggestions

The Accelerated Settlement Task Force (AST) has carefully planned and directed the UK's shift to a T+1 settlement cycle. Launched in December 2022, the AST played a key role in investigating and setting the groundwork for this momentous change. This chapter dives into the AST report, reviewing the focal areas such as operational improvements, communication methods, and timelines, and summarizing the ten main recommendations. It also outlines the duties and obligations of the Technical Group, has a thorough action plan with deadlines, and talks about Andrew Douglas's leadership style as the group chair.

A synopsis of the ten main suggestions

A comprehensive strategic plan for the UK's transition to T+1 was offered by the AST study. The following is a summary of the ten main recommendations:

Make a definite timeline

Establish a clear schedule for the switch to T+1 and make sure everyone in the market is informed and ready for it.

Modernize Your Technology Infrastructure

1. Require large capital expenditures in technology to facilitate the automation and real-time processing required for T+1.

Boosting Operational Procedures

1. Optimize and streamline operational processes to support the quicker settlement cycle.

Boost Channels of Communication

1. Create effective communication plans to inform and include all parties involved in the change.

Perform Thorough Testing

1. To guarantee preparedness, conduct comprehensive testing phases that include industry-wide rehearsals.

Comply with International Standards

1. To promote cross-border transactions and standardize settlement cycles, collaborate with foreign peers.

Offer Guidance and Assistance

Provide market participants with resources and training programs to assist them in adjusting to the new settlement cycle.

Observe and Assess

Create systems for ongoing observation and assessment after installation to quickly address any problems.

Promote cooperation

To guarantee a seamless transition, encourage cooperation between technology suppliers, regulatory agencies, and market players.

Create backup plans

Make backup arrangements to reduce any possible hazards and interruptions throughout the shift.

Priorities: Deadlines, Communication Strategies, and Operational Changes

According to the AST report, operational adjustments, communication plans, and deadline compliance are the three main areas of concentration that must be addressed for T+1 to be implemented successfully.

Modifications to Operations

Automation and Real-Time Processing: The AST emphasized that in order for market participants to meet the expectations of T+1, their systems must be upgraded. It also emphasized the necessity of automation and real-time processing. This covers trade confirmations, settlements, and reconciliations in real time.

Workflow Optimization: Re-engineering current workflows is necessary for the changeover. Procedures that required two days to complete now only take one day, requiring a major reorganization of how things are done.

Risk management To deal with the shorter settlement period, improved risk management frameworks need to be created. This entails tighter oversight and quicker handling of any inconsistencies or problems.

Techniques of Communication

Engaging Stakeholders: Good communication is essential. Frequent updates and forums where stakeholders can talk about advancements, difficulties, and solutions are advised by the AST.

Public Awareness efforts: Extensive public awareness efforts are required to guarantee that all market players, including smaller businesses and retail investors, are informed of the developments.

Feedback Mechanisms: Setting up routes for feedback enables prompt modifications and real-time resolution of issues.

Timelines

Phased Implementation: The AST suggested a methodical strategy, delineating distinct timeframes for every phase of the shift. This covers the dates of technology updates, testing stages, and complete deployment.

Milestone Reviews: Regular milestone reviews help to make sure the change is proceeding as planned. These evaluations make it possible to evaluate the state of affairs and pinpoint any areas in need of more care.

The role and responsibilities of the technical group

Andrew Douglas is the chair of the Technical Group, which is crucial to the T+1 implementation. This team is in charge of turning the AST's suggestions into doable actions and making sure that every facet of the transition is painstakingly planned out and carried out.

A thorough action plan with deadlines

Action Plan: The Technical Group created a thorough action plan that included deadlines, accountable parties, and specified activities. This strategy addresses every facet of the shift, including stakeholder communication, operational modifications, and technology advancements.

Timelines: Detailed timetables were created, complete with deadlines and benchmarks for every stage of the changeover. This methodical approach guarantees that every task is finished on time and that any possible delays are quickly resolved.

Observation and Assessment

1. The Technical Group is in charge of keeping an ongoing eye on the implementation procedure. This entails providing frequent updates on development, assessing test phases, and making the required modifications in response to criticism and results.

2. After implementation, the team will keep an eye on the market to make sure the T+1 settlement cycle runs smoothly and to handle any problems that may come up.

Douglas's Method of Leadership

As chair of the Technical Group, Andrew Douglas applies a strategic and cooperative approach honed from his vast experience in the post-trade sector. These are the qualities that define his leadership:

Strategic Perspective:

With an emphasis on long-term advantages like lower risk, increased market efficiency, and increased global competitiveness for the UK's financial markets, Douglas has a clear plan for the switch to T+1.

Collaborative Interaction

1. Douglas has made interacting with all stakeholders a top priority since he understands how important teamwork is. This inclusive strategy makes sure that different market participants' viewpoints and issues are taken into account.

2. Frequent forums, workshops, and meetings encourage candid communication and a sense of collective accountability for the transition's success.

Choosing Action:

1. Douglas is renowned for taking decisive action and advancing initiatives. His guidance makes sure that the changeover proceeds as planned and that any challenges are met head-on.

2. Douglas keeps everyone accountable and establishes clear expectations to make sure the implementation goes according to schedule.

Modifications to Operations

2024-2025: Workflows should be redesigned in 2024–2025 to account for the quicker settlement cycle. To guarantee that every employee is competent in the new procedures, offer training and assistance.

2025: Test operational readiness through industry-wide rehearses and simulations. Adapt according to test results to streamline processes.

Interaction and Communication

Continuous: Keep in constant contact with all parties involved. Provide progress reports, respond to queries, and solicit comments.

2024–2025: Start public awareness efforts and offer materials to inform market players about the T+1 transition.

Observance and Complying

2025: Put in place oversight procedures to guarantee adherence to new rules and guidelines. To gauge progress, do routine audits and reviews.

Post-Implementation: Maintain monitoring and assessment to make sure the T+1 settlement cycle runs smoothly and to take care of any new problems that may arise.

The process of getting ready for T+1 settlement to be implemented in the UK is intricate and multidimensional. A strategic roadmap is offered by the AST report and its suggestions, which concentrate on important topics including operational adjustments, communication tactics, and deadline observance. Under Andrew Douglas' direction, the Technical Group is essential to carrying out this strategy because they make sure that every detail of the transfer is well thought out and carried out. By use of a well-defined strategy, cooperative involvement, resolute measures, and an emphasis on novelty, the United Kingdom is well positioned to effectively execute the shift to T+1, augmenting the effectiveness, steadiness, and worldwide competitiveness of its financial markets.

Chapter 4

T+1 and Securities Finance

Securities Finance Market Dynamics

Lending and borrowing of securities to support trading strategies, liquidity management, and other financial activities is known as securities finance, and it is an essential part of the financial markets. The idea of this market's operation is to give short-term liquidity while facilitating market players' ability to fulfill their settlement responsibilities. Efficient collateral management, high trading volume, and quick transaction cycles define the dynamics of securities financing.

Given its current procedures and infrastructure, the securities finance market is particularly positioned to adjust in the context of the switch to a T+1 settlement cycle. The transition to T+1 necessitates even quicker processing times and stronger risk management systems, both of which are part and parcel of securities finance operations.

The Alignment of T+0 Trading with T+1

For many of its transactions, securities financing normally uses a T+0 (same-day settlement) basis. Due to this method, stocks and funds can be transferred right away because trades are settled the same day they are conducted. The necessity for effective collateral utilization and real-time liquidity is what essentially drives this quick settlement cycle.

There are various ways to view how T+0 trade and the T+1 settlement cycle align:

Efficiency and Speed: Systems and procedures that manage quick transaction cycles are already in place in the securities finance markets. By guaranteeing that all securities transactions are finalized within one business day, the switch to T+1 is a positive step toward greater market efficiency and fits in nicely with the rapidity of T+0 trading.

Risk management: To reduce counterparty and operational risks, T+0 trading necessitates strict risk management procedures. These risk management frameworks will remain essential to the seamless settlement of trades within the abbreviated cycle as the market moves toward T+1.

Technological Infrastructure: Real-time transaction confirmation, collateral management, and settlement are supported by an advanced technological infrastructure necessary for T+0 trading. This infrastructure can easily adjust to T+1 because the current systems are already designed with efficiency and speed in mind.

Provision of Liquidity: A crucial component of securities financing is the capacity to supply and oversee liquidity. Market players can gain quicker access to funds and securities with T+1, which improves the overall stability and liquidity of the market.

The Adaptation Strategies of EquiLend and Their Client Readiness

Leading post-trade solutions supplier to the securities financing sector, EquiLend, has taken the initiative to get ready for the switch to T+1. A smooth transition depends on the firm's adaption plans and client preparedness programs.

Technological Advancements

EquiLend has made considerable investments to modernize its IT infrastructure in order to facilitate the T+1 settlement cycle. These improvements include better system integration with market players, real-time data processing, and sophisticated automation.

Adjustments for operations

EquiLend has adjusted its operational workflows to conform to T+1. This entails expediting trade confirmation, settlement, and collateral management procedures to guarantee timely and effective processing of all transactions.

Instruction and Assistance for Clients

Complete training programs have been introduced by EquiLend to get its clients ready for T+1. The new operating processes, technology needs, and best practices for transition management are all covered in these programs. EquiLend also offers materials and ongoing support to help clients adjust to the changes.

Compliance and Risk Management

In order to guarantee that all transactions under T+1 are carried out with the least amount of risk possible, EquiLend has reinforced its risk management systems. To handle any potential disruptions, this entails strong contingency plans, real-time risk assessment, and improved monitoring.

Industry Cooperation

EquiLend regularly interacts with industry stakeholders, regulatory agencies, and technology vendors because it understands the value of teamwork. By working together, we can make sure that the change to T+1 is seamless and well-coordinated by ensuring that it adheres to industry best practices and standards.

The securities finance industry has opportunities as well as challenges with the shift to a T+1 settlement cycle. The current T+0 trading procedures in securities finance, with their focus on speed, efficiency, and strong risk management, offer a strong basis for this shift. EquiLend is in a good position to handle this transition thanks to its proactive adaptation tactics and extensive client readiness programs, which guarantee that its clients can easily adjust to the new settlement cycle. The securities finance sector stands to gain from increased liquidity, lower risk, and improved operational efficiency as the market shifts towards T+1. These factors will support the stability and competitiveness of the financial markets as a whole.

Chapter 5

Implementing Projects and Orders

Important Modifications to Operations

The financial industry will need to make significant operational adjustments in order to switch to a T+1 settlement period. There are several obstacles and chances to increase efficiency associated with this transition from a T+2 cycle, which permits trade settlement in two business days, to a T+1 cycle, which necessitates settlement the following business day.

Technological Upgrades and Process Modifications

Automated Systems and Real-Time Processing

Automation: To meet the demands of T+1, financial institutions must heavily invest in automation. This involves deploying sophisticated systems capable of handling high volumes of trades with minimal manual intervention. Automated trade matching, confirmation, and settlement processes are essential.

Real-Time Data Processing: Real-time data processing and reporting are crucial. Institutions must ensure their systems can process, validate, and report trades in real time to meet the accelerated deadlines. This requires upgrades to both hardware and software infrastructures.

Improved Networks for Communication

SWIFT Messaging: The quick and safe exchange of trade and settlement instructions depends on the incorporation of SWIFT messaging standards. Improvements made to communication networks guarantee prompt confirmation and transmission of communications.

Blockchain Technology: In order to improve transparency and enable real-time transactions, some businesses are investigating blockchain technology. The decentralized ledger technology of blockchain can offer a safe, immediate record of transactions.

Strong Risk Management Frameworks

Effective management of intraday liquidity is crucial due to the abbreviated settlement cycle. Real-time monitoring and management of liquidity levels is crucial for firms to prevent settlement failures.

Risk Monitoring and Mitigation: To quickly identify, track, and reduce settlement risks, enhanced risk management frameworks are needed. This includes emergency preparation and real-time risk assessment tools.

Reengineering Workflows

Streamlined Processes: To cut down on processing times and eliminate inefficiencies, current processes must be redesigned. This entails outlining every stage of the trade processing process and pinpointing areas in need of development.

Centralized clearing and settlement: Standardizing procedures and lowering settlement risks can be achieved by utilizing centralized clearing and settlement services. For trades to be settled quickly and securely, central counterparties, or CCPs, are essential.

Mandatory Modifications to Operations Commencing in 2025

Starting in 2025, the UK government and regulatory agencies have mandated a number of operational modifications to ensure a seamless transition to T+1. The purpose of these requirements is to guarantee that all parties involved in the market are ready for the upcoming settlement cycle.

Adherence to Regulations

Mandatory Reporting: Organizations must notify regulatory agencies of their preparedness and adherence to T+1 mandates. To guarantee conformity, routine audits and compliance checks will be carried out.

Standardized Procedures: Timeliness and standardized procedures for trade settlement will be enforced by regulations. One aspect of this is standardizing settlement practices among various asset classes and market players.

Application of Technology:

System updates: Financial institutions have deadlines for completing the essential technology updates. This entails modernizing risk management frameworks, communication networks, and trade processing technologies.

Testing and Certification: To guarantee that they satisfy the T+1 standards, all systems and procedures must go through a thorough testing and certification process. Firms may be required by regulatory organizations to take part in industry-wide testing phases.

Adjustments for operations:

Reduced Settlement timeframes: In order to comply with the T+1 cycle, firms need to modify their operational timeframes. In order to guarantee that trades are confirmed, matched, and settled within the new timeframe, procedures must be put in place.

Employee Training: Sufficient training initiatives are needed to guarantee that employees are knowledgeable on the newest procedures and technological advancements. Sustained instruction and assistance will be essential for efficient operations.

Case Studies of Pioneers in the Field

Numerous companies have initiated the T+1 implementation process, offering significant perspectives on the obstacles and optimal methodologies linked to this shift.

Investment Bank A Case Study

Investment Bank as the implementation strategy A began investing in cutting-edge automation technology in order to get ready for T+1. They created a proprietary automated transaction processing system that matched and settled trades in real time.

Problems and Solutions: The main issue was figuring out how to integrate the new system with the pre-existing legacy systems. The bank used a phased implementation strategy to overcome this, progressively transferring various asset classes to the new system. This made it possible to test and make adjustments continuously without interfering with current activities.

Results: The bank significantly decreased settlement failure rates and settlement timeframes, which raised operational effectiveness and decreased risk.

Asset Management Firm B Case Study

Implementation Strategy: Asset Management Firm B's implementation strategy centered on improving coordination and communication with its counterparties and custodians. They put in place a strong SWIFT messaging infrastructure to guarantee smooth collaboration.

Problems and Solutions: Making sure all counterparties were equally ready for T+1 was one of the major problems. In order to harmonize its procedures with those of its counterparties, the company arranged cooperative testing sessions and workshops.

Results: By working together, the market players were able to synchronize the change with minimal disruptions and increased trust.

Case Study: Company C Brokerage

Implementation Strategy: To enable real-time settlements, Brokerage Firm C made use of blockchain technology. They collaborated with a blockchain technology supplier to create a trade settlement decentralized ledger system.

Problems and Solutions: The primary issue was the lack of clarity in the regulations pertaining to blockchain technology. In order to guarantee compliance and obtain the required permissions, the firm maintained tight ties with regulatory agencies.

Results: By offering unmatched security and transparency, the blockchain technology drastically cut down on operating expenses and settlement times.

Perspectives from Companies Using T+1

Early adopters' experiences provide other businesses getting ready for T+1 with several important insights:

It's Important to Prepare Early: By implementing process reengineering and technology upgrades early on, possible issues can be recognized and resolved well in advance of the official changeover.

Working together and Communication: Aseamless transition depends on efficient coordination and communication with all parties involved, including counterparties, custodians, and regulators. Process alignment and cooperative testing help stop interruptions.

Phased Implementation: Businesses can manage risks and make necessary modifications gradually by using a phased implementation approach. This promotes continual improvement and reduces operational disturbances.

Flexibility and Innovation: Using cutting-edge technology like automation and blockchain can give you a competitive advantage. On the other hand, adaptability and the ability to adjust to changes in regulations are equally crucial.

Constant Monitoring and Support: Sustaining compliance and operational efficiency is ensured by constant monitoring of systems and procedures as well as by giving employees ongoing training and assistance.

Big operational tasks and mandates are involved in the switch to T+1 settlement. Improved communication networks, process adjustments, and technology advancements are some of the major operational changes. All market participants will be ready and able to comply with the new settlement cycle thanks to mandated operational adjustments that will take effect in 2025. Early adopters offer insightful case studies that emphasize the significance of early planning, teamwork, phased implementation, and innovation. Financial institutions may ensure a competitive edge in the dynamic financial sector, improve efficiency, lower risks, and successfully navigate the transition to T+1 by utilizing these insights.

Chapter 6

Interaction and Arrangement

Strategies for Cross-European Communication

The shift to a T+1 settlement cycle is a difficult procedure that calls for efficient coordination and communication amongst numerous European parties. The financial markets are interrelated, thus effective communication tactics that promote smooth information sharing and teamwork are critical to the success of this shift.

Identified Communication Protocols

Unified Messaging Standards: All market participants can communicate information reliably and effectively by putting in place standardized communication protocols, like SWIFT messaging. In a T+1 setting when time is of the importance, this standardization reduces mistakes and misunderstandings.

Real-Time Data Sharing: Encouraging trade reporting and real-time data sharing through the use of technology helps to keep things transparent and ensures that everyone is in agreement. It is imperative to have platforms that offer real-time updates on transaction statuses, confirmations, and settlements.

Frequent Meetings for Coordination

Industry Forums and Working Groups: To promote continuous communication and problem-solving, financial institutions, regulators, and technology providers should form frequent forums and working groups. These teams are able to work together to solve problems, exchange information, and create best practices.

Regulatory Consultations: Ensuring that all market players are aware of compliance obligations and impending changes requires ongoing engagement with regulatory organizations. Frequent discussions aid in bringing industry operations into compliance with deadlines and expectations set by regulations.

Education and Training: Workshops and Webinars: Market participants can learn about new procedures, technologies, and compliance needs by hosting workshops and webinars centered around T+1 settlement. These meetings can answer any questions or concerns and offer helpful insights.

Guidelines and Manuals: Creating thorough guidelines and manuals that describe the stages involved in T+1 settlement can be very helpful to market players as reference tools. These materials ought to be readily available and updated on a regular basis.

Joint Ventures Throughout European Regions
Given the complexity and diversity of Europe's financial markets, cross-jurisdictional cooperation is essential to a smooth transition to T+1. Market efficiency can be improved and practices harmonized by European countries working together.

Work Groups Across Europe

Joint Task Forces: To guarantee a coordinated approach to T+1 implementation, joint task forces comprising individuals from several European nations should be formed. These task forces can resolve cross-border issues, standardize operational methods, and coordinate regulatory frameworks.

Technical Committees: More focused and efficient solutions may result from the creation of technical committees to address particular facets of the shift, such as risk assessment, technology integration, and operational modifications.

Commonly Used Best Practices

Experience Sharing: Promoting the sharing of firsthand knowledge and lessons discovered by T+1 early adopters might yield insightful information. Case studies and success stories can assist other jurisdictions in avoiding typical mistakes and putting into practice sensible tactics.

Benchmarking: Comparing the development and preparedness of other jurisdictions through benchmarking exercises can highlight areas for development and promote a constructive climate of rivalry and cooperation.

Coordinated Timelines

Coordinated Implementation timetables: To avoid inconsistencies and guarantee a seamless transition, implementation timetables should be aligned amongst European states. A coordinated strategy reduces the possibility of operational hiccups and improves market stability.

Uniform Deadlines: To make sure that everyone in the market is aiming for the same goals, uniform deadlines should be established for important milestones like system upgrades and regulatory compliance. This alignment aids in lowering uncertainty and controlling expectations.

The Value of Coordinated Schedules and Exchanged Best Practices

Mutually agreed upon timetables and best practices must be followed in order for T+1 settlement to be implemented successfully. Cohesion and coordination among market participants and jurisdictions create a positive environment that benefits the whole financial ecosystem when they work toward common goals with synchronized schedules.

Reducing Interruptions to Operations

Timelines that are synchronized ensure that everyone moves to T+1 at the same time, reducing operational disturbances. By coordinating, gaps and overlaps that can result in market instability or settlement failures are avoided.

Increasing Market Self-Belief

Market trust is raised by a consistent strategy to T+1 deployment, which shows that the industry is organized and well-prepared. By offering a path forward, shared best practices foster trust in the strength and dependability of the new settlement cycle.

Enhancing The Allocation of Resources

Market participants can concentrate on tried-and-true tactics and solutions when coordinated efforts and best practices are shared. This maximizes resource allocation. This effectiveness guarantees that resources are employed efficiently to accomplish shared goals and minimizes duplication of effort.

Encouraging Harmonization of Regulations

Regulatory harmonization is promoted by harmonizing schedules and processes across countries, which makes it simpler for businesses to comply with cross-border regulations. Smoother international operations are made possible by this harmonization, which lowers the complexity and costs of compliance.

For Europe to successfully move to T+1 settlement, efficient cooperation and communication are essential. European jurisdictions may guarantee a seamless and effective transition by putting in place uniform communication protocols, encouraging teamwork, and aligning deadlines. Coordinated efforts and common best practices reduce operational disruptions while also boosting market harmony and regulatory coherence. These tactics will be crucial to preserving the integrity and stability of Europe's financial markets as it transitions to T+1.

Chapter 7

The Road to T+1 in Europe

ESMA's Request for Proof

The regulatory environment governing the European financial markets is significantly shaped by the European Securities and Markets Authority (ESMA). ESMA released a Call for Evidence in March 2024 as part of its proactive stance toward the possible switch to a T+1 settlement cycle. The objective of this endeavor was to collect thorough input from industry associations, investors, financial institutions, and other relevant parties in order to evaluate the viability, consequences, and preparedness of this kind of change throughout the European Union.

Goals of the Evidence Request

Evaluating Market Readiness: Find out how ready different market players are for the shift to T+1.

Identifying Challenges: Determine any operational, technological, or legal issues that may come up as a result of the change.

Benefits Evaluation: Recognize the possible advantages, including improved competitiveness, lower risk, and increased efficiency.

Cost-Benefit Analysis: To determine the entire impact on the European financial market, perform a thorough cost-benefit analysis.

Market Responses and Their Consequences

A variety of viewpoints were presented in the answer to ESMA's Call for Evidence, which reflected the diversity of the European financial markets.

Positive Reactions

Operational Efficiency: A number of respondents emphasized that by cutting the time required to settle deals, the T+1 cycle might result in considerable operational efficiencies, freeing up cash and lowering counterparty risk.

Risk Reduction: It was thought that shortening the settlement cycle would help lower counterparty and operational risks, which would improve the stability of the financial system.

Global Competitiveness: It was believed that staying in line with economies like the US, Canada, and Mexico, which are transitioning to T+1, would help to draw in foreign investment and preserve global competitiveness.

Issues Voiced

Technology changes: The technology changes needed to support T+1 have drawn significant criticism. Particularly smaller institutions were concerned about the expenses and intricacy involved in putting these reforms into effect.

Operational disturbances: One of the main worries was the possibility of operational disturbances during the shift. Participants in the market stressed the importance of a carefully thought-out, staggered deployment strategy.

Regulatory and Compliance Issues: One of the biggest challenges was making sure that all market players complied with the latest rules and guidelines. Clear norms and regulatory body assistance were demanded.

Comprehensive Cost-Benefit Analysis

Technological Investments: Significant sums of money must be spent on new hardware, software, and infrastructure in order to upgrade current systems to enable T+1 settlement. These expenses cover both the original investment and continuing upkeep and improvements.

Training and Development: It costs a lot to train employees to adjust to new procedures and systems. Programs for ongoing education will be required to guarantee that every employee is knowledgeable about the new T+1 criteria.

Operational Adjustments: Businesses will have to restructure their operational processes, which may entail bringing on more employees or reallocating funds. While staff members adjust to new protocols, productivity may temporarily decline.

Advantages

Diminished Risk: By cutting the settlement cycle to T+1, the likelihood of a counterparty default between the trade date and settlement date is decreased, hence reducing counterparty risk. This improves the financial market's general stability.

Enhanced Efficiency: Using money and resources more effectively is the result of quicker settlement cycles. It enables businesses to enhance liquidity management and reallocate funds more swiftly.

Competitive Advantage: Europe's competitiveness is increased by aligning with global economies that have already made the switch to T+1. This could draw in more foreign investment and strengthen economic relations.

Possibility of Alignment with Europe

There is a good chance that European jurisdictions will align on the T+1 transition, based on the input and the thorough research. Strategic planning and well-coordinated activities are essential for a smooth transition.

Europe's Strategic Recommendations

Phased Implementation: The danger of operational disruptions can be reduced by implementing T+1 in stages. Before a full-scale rollout, the first stages could entail pilot programs with a small number of market players to evaluate and improve processes.

Regulatory Support: To assist market players in meeting new standards, regulatory bodies should offer clear guidance, resources, and support. This offers access to professional consultations, compliance checklists, and comprehensive timetables.

Fostering collaboration between financial institutions and technology suppliers can facilitate the development of standardized solutions that have the potential to be broadly adopted. Partnerships and joint ventures can lower expenses while advancing technology.

Engagement with Stakeholders: It is imperative to maintain constant communication with all stakeholders, including investors, trade associations, and financial institutions. Frequent updates, feedback meetings, and group problem-solving projects can guarantee a seamless and inclusive transition.

Potential for a Combined T+1 Transition Schedule

Encouraging extensive cooperation among all parties and careful preparation are necessary to achieve a consistent T+1 transition schedule throughout Europe.

Cooperation Among Jurisdictions: It is imperative that European jurisdictions work together to harmonize their transition schedules and legal structures. By aligning, disparities are reduced and uniform standards are followed by all market players.

Harmonized dates: All stakeholders' activities are better coordinated when critical milestones like staff training, regulatory compliance, and technology improvements have harmonized dates. This cohesive strategy can guarantee a smooth transition and avoid fragmentation.

Monitoring and Assessment: It's critical to set up systems for ongoing observation and assessment of the transition process. Frequent evaluations can help spot possible problems early and enable prompt action to keep the transformation moving forward.

Europe faces numerous opportunities as well as problems on the road to T+1 resolution. While acknowledging the intricacy of the change, ESMA's Call for Evidence and the thorough input from industry players also draw attention to its possible advantages in terms of effectiveness, lower risk, and increased competitiveness internationally. A successful transition requires a planned, staged strategy backed by strong technology and regulatory frameworks. Europe can efficiently navigate the path to T+1 by coordinating schedules and exchanging best practices, guaranteeing a stable and functioning financial industry that is resilient on the international scene.

Chapter 8

Takeaways from Europe and the US

Comparative Evaluation
Because of the disparate regulatory environments, market configurations, and operational dynamics in the US and Europe, the transition to a T+1 settlement cycle has transpired in diverse ways. Comparative study of these areas provides important information on tactics, obstacles, and achievements that can guide international implementation initiatives.

Variations in Strategies for Implementation
Regulatory Strategies

United States: With a strict regulatory mandate, the US Securities and Exchange Commission (SEC) led the charge in the move to T+1. The SEC established precise timelines and supplied comprehensive rules to guarantee adherence by all market players. The enforcement procedures and strict regulatory scrutiny that typified this top-down approach.

Europe: By releasing a Call for Evidence to solicit input from market participants prior to proposing specific remedies, the European Securities and Markets Authority (ESMA), on the other hand, used a more consultative approach. A more gradual and consensus-driven transformation was made possible by this technique, which placed an emphasis on inclusivity and collaboration.

The state of the market and participant readiness

United States: A more coordinated deployment was made possible by the highly consolidated US financial industry, which has fewer large financial institutions and major exchanges. The change was further accelerated by the availability of strong infrastructure and cutting-edge technology skills among important companies.

Europe: With numerous exchanges and a wide variety of financial institutions that differ in size and technological competence, Europe's financial industry is more fragmented. Due to this variability, establishing uniform readiness was made more difficult and required customized solutions to account for varying levels of preparedness.

Infrastructure and Technology

United States: Long before the official transition, US institutions profited from significant expenditures in infrastructure and technology. An easier transition to T+1 was made possible by the advanced risk management frameworks, automated systems, and real-time data processing that were already in place.

Europe: Although prominent European institutions made technological investments as well, there were notable differences in overall preparedness. Upgrades to systems and procedures were challenging for smaller institutions in particular, underscoring the need for support and staggered implementation techniques.

Comparabilities Among Implementation Techniques
Engaging Stakeholders

Stakeholder involvement was given top priority in both the US and Europe because of the realization that it is crucial to include every market participant in the transformation process. To handle issues and get feedback, cooperative working groups, regular discussions, and feedback sessions were often used tactics.

Staged Execution

In order to reduce risks and guarantee a seamless transition, a staged strategy was used in both regions. Pilot projects, testing stages, and phased rollouts made it possible to make ongoing adjustments and improvements based on practical experience.

Put Risk Management First

In both the US and Europe, improving risk management frameworks was a major area of concern. Robust systems for intraday liquidity management, real-time risk assessment, and contingency planning to address settlement failures were necessary to shorten the settlement cycle.

Important Takeaways and Worldwide Uses

A number of important lessons can be drawn from the US and Europe's experiences moving to T+1 that can be implemented successfully in other areas of the world.

Regulatory Support and Clarity
Explicit Rules and Timelines

Ensuring that all market players are aware of the criteria and timetables requires the establishment of precise regulatory standards and deadlines. This clarity promotes coordinated efforts toward compliance and aids in creating reasonable expectations.

Worldwide Use: Global regulatory agencies have to furnish comprehensive timetables and structures for the execution of T+1, guaranteeing that all concerned parties are apprised and equipped.

Regulatory Assistance and Cooperation

In order to handle difficulties and guarantee seamless transitions, regulatory organizations provide ongoing support through workshops, consultations, and compliance assistance.

Global Application: In order to foster confidence and compliance, regulators should actively collaborate with market participants, providing direction and support during the transition process.

Technology Readiness

Investing in the latest technology

Infrastructure and significant technological investments are needed to enable the quicker settlement cycle. Important elements include sophisticated risk management tools, real-time data processing, and automated systems.

Worldwide Use: Global financial institutions ought to place a high priority on technology advancements and make investments in scalable systems that can manage the higher transaction volumes and complexities brought on by T+1.

Gradual Releases and Evaluations

Institutions can test and improve their systems and procedures gradually by implementing T+1 in phases. Testing phases and pilot programs aid in the early detection of problems and the implementation of the required corrections.

Global Application: Areas contemplating T+1 ought to execute staged rollouts, beginning with pilot projects involving important industry players and progressively growing to full-scale deployment in response to test findings and input.

Collaboration and Involvement of Stakeholders
Engaging All Stakeholders Inclusively

Incorporating all relevant parties, such as financial institutions, trade associations, technology suppliers, and investors, guarantees that a range of viewpoints are taken into account and addressed. This all-inclusive strategy encourages teamwork and group problem-solving.

Global Application: To ensure widespread support and alignment during the T+1 transition process, countries and regions should set up forums, working groups, and frequent consultations.

Cross-Border Arrangement

Cross-border coordination is necessary to establish harmonized practices and prevent disparities in regions with interconnected marketplaces. Timelines, norms, and legal structures that are consistent across jurisdictions can improve productivity and stability.

Global Application: In order to achieve a coordinated global transition to T+1, regulatory agencies and market participants must work together internationally. This is especially true in regions where there is a substantial amount of cross-border trading activity.

Improvements in Risk Management
Sturdy Risk Management Structures

Reducing the risks related to shorter settlement cycles requires the development and application of strong risk management frameworks. Key elements include contingency planning and real-time risk assessment systems.

Global Application: To mitigate the risk of settlement failures, financial institutions worldwide should improve their risk management procedures, emphasizing intraday liquidity management, real-time monitoring, and strong backup plans.

Constant observation and development

Prompt identification and resolution of difficulties is facilitated by ongoing monitoring and evaluation of the implementation process. Sturdy efficiency and stability are ensured by ongoing improvement based on input and practical experience.

Global Application: To enable quick modifications and enhancements in response to changing demands and problems, regions implementing T+1 should set up systems for ongoing monitoring and reporting.

Many lessons from the US and Europe's transition to T+1 settlement can be used globally. The significance of stakeholder participation, technology readiness, legislative clarity, and strong risk management frameworks are among the most important lessons learned. Through the application of these lessons, additional regions will be better equipped to manage the challenges associated with T+1 implementation, resulting in more seamless transitions and an overall improvement in the efficiency and stability of the world's financial markets. A coordinated and effective worldwide transition to T+1 will be made possible by these shared experiences and best practices, especially as the globe moves toward faster settlement cycles

Chapter 9

Settlers Cycles' Future

Forecasts and Patterns

The financial markets are always changing due to changes in market dynamics, regulatory reforms, and technology improvements. Investigating possible future trends and the development of settlement cycles beyond T+1 is crucial as the industry adjusts to the T+1 settlement cycle. This chapter explores the outlook for settlement cycles as well as the technological advancements that could influence trade in the future.

Development Past T+1

Proceeding with the Same-Day Settlement (T+0)

Immediate Settlement: T+0, or same-day settlement of transactions, is the ultimate objective for many in the financial sector. Liquidity would be increased and settlement risk would be all but eliminated. Significant technological developments and adjustments to operational procedures would be necessary to achieve T+0.

Global Impact: By boosting productivity and cutting down on the amount of time capital is held hostage throughout the settlement process, same-day settlement has the potential to completely transform international trade. But there are significant obstacles to this shift in terms of technology, regulations, and international market coordination.

Ongoing Settlement

Real-Time Settlement: Continuous settlement, in which trades are settled in real-time all day long, is another possible development. A highly developed infrastructure that could process trades quickly as they happen would be necessary for this strategy.

Distributed ledger technology (DLT) and blockchain: By offering a safe, open, and decentralized platform for real-time transaction processing, these technologies have the potential to provide continuous settlement.

Reduced Cycles for Particular Asset Classes

Customized Settlement Cycles: These may be advantageous for certain asset classes. To suit differing operating needs and hazards, more traditional asset classes may stay at T+1 or T+2, while high-frequency trading and other fast-paced market segments may shift towards T+0.

Regulatory Flexibility: In order to balance the advantages of speed with the requirements for stability and risk management, regulatory frameworks would need to adjust to permit distinct settlement cycles for different asset classes.

The Impact of Technological Innovations

The evolution of settlement cycles in the future will be largely driven by technological advancements. Blockchain, machine learning, artificial intelligence (AI), and other technological advancements have the potential to completely change the trading and settlement environment.

Distributed ledger technology with blockchain

Enhanced Security and Transparency: Blockchain technology can offer an unchangeable, transparent ledger of transactions, lowering the possibility of fraud and boosting confidence among market players. Through transaction verification that is both secure and automated, this technology can help expedite the settlement process.

Smart Contracts: Using blockchain technology, smart contracts can automate post-trade and settlement procedures, guaranteeing that transactions are carried out and resolved in accordance with predetermined guidelines without the need for middlemen. Operational expenses and settlement times may be greatly decreased as a result.

Learning Machines and Artificial Intelligence:

Predictive analytics: By analyzing enormous volumes of data, artificial intelligence (AI) and machine learning can forecast market patterns and improve trading tactics. Because these tools may detect possible settlement problems before they arise, they can help improve risk management.

Automation and Efficiency: AI-driven automation can minimize manual intervention and error-prone back-office procedures. By learning from past data and adjusting to new trends, machine learning algorithms may continuously enhance these processes.

Computing in Quantum

Unprecedented Processing Power: With its enormous processing capacity, quantum computing, which is still in its early stages, has the potential to completely transform the financial markets. Potentially enabling real-time global settlement, quantum computers may handle massive amounts of transactions at previously unheard-of rates and solve intricate calculations.

Risk Management and Optimization: By streamlining portfolio management and risk assessment, quantum algorithms can offer more insightful and potent settlement risk management techniques.

Open Banking and API Integration

Collaboration and Interoperability: Application Programming Interfaces (APIs) and open banking principles can be combined to improve communication between various financial platforms and systems. This can make settlement procedures go more smoothly and quickly by allowing market players to collaborate and exchange data seamlessly.

Customization and Innovation: APIs make it possible to create solutions that are specifically suited to the demands of the market. The ability to be flexible can spur innovation in settlement procedures, increasing their effectiveness and ability to adapt to shifting market conditions.

The Path Ahead: Strategic Points to Remember
Future developments in the financial industry will be shaped by a number of strategic factors as it uses technology advancements and shorter settlement cycles.

Adjustment to Regulations

Global Coordination: Global regulatory authorities will need to work together in order to reduce settlement times even further. To guarantee a smooth and safe transition, it is essential to harmonize laws and standards between jurisdictions.

Flexible Frameworks: In order to keep up with the quick pace of technology innovation and the changing nature of market activities, regulatory frameworks must be flexible. This entails setting up pilot programs and sandboxes to test novel ideas and technologies in regulated settings.

Investments in Infrastructure

System Upgrades: To enable quicker settlement cycles, large investments in infrastructure and technology are necessary. Upgrading their systems must be a top priority for financial institutions in order to handle more complicated and volume transactions.

Resilience and Security: It is crucial to guarantee the financial infrastructure's resilience and security. In order to guard against potential attacks and interruptions, this entails putting strong cybersecurity measures and disaster recovery plans into action.

Readiness of Market Participants

Education and Training: To make sure market participants are ready for new settlement cycles and technologies, ongoing education and training programs are essential. This entails being aware of the effects of advancements like as blockchain and artificial intelligence.

Change Management: To help institutions through the shift, effective change management techniques are essential. This entails effective communication, including stakeholders, and providing support networks to deal with issues and difficulties.

Creativity and Cooperation

Public-Private Partnerships: Working together, public organizations (central banks, regulators) and private organizations (banks, fintech companies) may spur innovation and guarantee the efficacy and security of innovative settlement models.

Research and Development: To investigate new technologies and strategies that can further improve the effectiveness and security of settlement procedures, ongoing investment in research and development is required.

Due to changing market dynamics and technology improvements, settlement cycles are expected to undergo a major alteration in the future. Transitioning from T+1 to same-day or continuous settlement offers significant benefits in terms of heightened global competitiveness, less risk, and increased efficiency. However, achieving this goal will need concerted governmental actions, large infrastructural investments, and a dedication to innovation and cooperation on the part of all market players. The financial sector may set new norms for international financial markets by paving the path for a more effective, safe, and dynamic trading environment by utilizing technologies like blockchain, artificial intelligence, and quantum computing.

Chapter 10

T+1's Economic Consequences

Effects on the World Economy

The transition of the financial markets to a T+1 settlement cycle is a big deal that will have a big impact on the world economy. The economic advantages and difficulties of T+1 are examined in this chapter, along with a case study on how it would affect the US economy in 2024 and more general market ramifications such how it will affect investor behavior, market liquidity, and risk management.

Financial Gains
Enhanced Efficiency of the Market

Diminished Settlement Risk: The risk of unsettled deals, including counterparty risk, is greatly diminished by cutting the settlement cycle from T+2 to T+1. This improves investor confidence and market stability.

Faster Capital Reinvestment: As monies involved in the settlement process are released sooner, quicker settlement cycles provide faster capital reinvestment. This has the potential to increase market liquidity and encourage greater trading.

Enhanced Accessibility:

Increased Trading Volumes: As cash becomes available more quickly, players in the market can make more deals in the same amount of time, which could result in increased trading volumes and more dynamic markets.

Better Market Access: Shorter settlement times might draw in additional participants, such as smaller institutions and ordinary investors, who would have been turned off by the lengthier times.

Cuts in Costs

Reduced operating Costs: Financial institutions may see a decrease in operating costs as a result of streamlined settlement procedures. Reconciliations and manual intervention requirements are reduced, which boosts productivity and lowers costs.

Decreased Margin Requirements: Shorter settlement cycles reduce the need for substantial margin requirements to be maintained over long periods of time, freeing up cash for other purposes.

Financial Difficulties
Investments in infrastructure and technology

High Initial Costs: Making the switch to T+1 necessitates large infrastructure and technology investments. To accommodate more transactions and faster processing times, financial institutions must modernize their systems.

Ongoing Maintenance: In order to keep these systems safe and effective, regular upgrades and maintenance are required, which raises the operational expenses.

Adjustments for Operations and Compliance:

Training and Adaptation: Staff members must receive training in order to handle new procedures and technological advancements. Time and resources are needed for this, and efficiency may be momentarily impacted by a learning curve.

Regulatory Compliance: Financial institutions are required to make sure that the new T+1 regulations are followed. This calls for the potentially resource-intensive update of policies, procedures, and documentation.

Enhanced Needs for Intraday Liquidity:

Liquidity Management: To satisfy the requirements of T+1 settlements, institutions must more skillfully manage their intraday liquidity. This can be difficult, especially for smaller organizations with tighter budgets.

Risk of Settlement Failures: Although the shorter cycle lowers risk overall, if liquidity is not managed appropriately, the requirement for exact timing raises the chance of settlement failures.

Examining T+1's Impact on the US Economy in 2024

The US's move to T+1 settlement in 2024 is a specific illustration of how this change would affect the economy.

An increase in market activity

Increased Trading Volumes: The US markets experienced a discernible rise in trading volume after the switch. Market activity was increased by traders being able to complete more transactions in a shorter amount of time thanks to the quicker settlement cycle.

Enhanced Investor Confidence: More institutional and retail investors participated as a result of the settlement risk being reduced, which raised investor confidence.

Gains in Operational Efficiency

Cost reductions: As a result of lower operating overheads, major financial institutions claimed considerable cost reductions. These reductions were a result of reduced human reconciliations and automated procedures.

Problems and Changes

Liquidity Management: To satisfy the requirements of T+1, financial institutions had to modify their strategies for managing liquidity. This entailed making sure there was enough liquidity on hand for settlements as well as maximizing cash flows.

Regulatory Compliance: Although there were early difficulties, making the necessary changes to internal policies and procedures to ensure compliance with new legislation resulted in more effective compliance frameworks.

Broader implications for the market
Liquidity in the Market

Instant Fund Availability: A settlement's faster money release improves market liquidity as a whole. Because they can reinvest their wealth more quickly, investors help to create a lively and active market.

Draw in New Participants: Shorter settlement cycles may have turned off smaller investors and institutions, but improved liquidity circumstances may draw in new players.

Risk Control

Reduction of Counterparty Risk: Shorter settlement cycles improve overall market stability by drastically reducing the amount of time counterparties are exposed to risk.

Enhanced Risk Management Practices: To meet the needs of T+1, financial institutions are urged to implement more advanced risk management techniques. This includes enhanced liquidity management techniques and real-time monitoring.

Investor Conduct:

An increase in trading frequency among investors may result from the opportunity to settle trades more quickly. Increased market activity and possibly additional profit-making chances may follow from this.

Increased Market Confidence: Investor confidence is bolstered by the decreased settlement risk, which may stimulate increased participation and market expansion.

Technological Progress:

Innovation and Development: As financial organizations look to modernize their systems and procedures, the shift to T+1 spurs technical innovation. New platforms and technologies that further improve market efficiency may result from this.

Adoption of Advanced Technologies: In order to facilitate quicker settlement cycles, technologies like blockchain, artificial intelligence, and machine learning are becoming more and more crucial, which is propelling further breakthroughs in these fields.

The transition to a T+1 settlement cycle is a major advancement in the development of financial markets, bringing with it a host of financial advantages including improved liquidity, lower costs, and higher market efficiency. It does, however, also come with drawbacks, such as the requirement for large technology expenditures, modifications to operations, and efficient liquidity management.

These advantages and difficulties are demonstrated by the example study of the US's shift to T+1 in 2024, emphasizing the significance of planning, flexibility, and creativity. The lessons from the US experience can offer helpful direction as other regions contemplate such transformations.

T+1 has significant wider market ramifications that affect investor behavior, risk management, and market liquidity. T+1 promotes increased market trust and efficiency, which opens the door to a more resilient and dynamic global financial system. Future trading will be further shaped by the industry's pursuit of even shorter settlement cycles and the use of cutting-edge technologies, which will propel further advancements in market stability and performance.

Chapter 11

The Role of Technology in T+1

Technological Enablers

The transition to a T+1 settlement cycle heavily relies on advanced technologies that streamline processes and enhance efficiencies. Critical technologies facilitating T+1 include:

Blockchain Technology:

Decentralized Ledger: Blockchain provides a secure, transparent, and immutable ledger for recording transactions, reducing the need for intermediaries and speeding up the settlement process.

Smart Contracts: By eliminating human error and increasing reliability, automated agreement execution via smart contracts guarantees accurate and quick trade settlement.

Innovations in Fintech

Artificial Intelligence (AI) and Machine Learning: Through real-time dataset analysis, AI and machine learning algorithms can improve risk management, detect settlement failures, and optimize trade matching.

Robotic Process Automation (RPA): RPA reduces manual intervention and speeds up settlement procedures by automating repetitive operations like data entry and reconciliation.

Systems for Real-Time Gross Settlement (RTGS) Instantaneous Settlements: Real-time fund and securities transfers are made possible by RTGS systems, which lowers the risk of delayed settlements by guaranteeing prompt settlement of transactions.

APIs, or application programming interfaces: Seamless Integration: APIs make it possible for diverse financial systems to integrate with one another in a seamless manner. This promotes effective data interchange and platform compatibility, both of which are necessary for the quick completion of T+1 settlements.

The Significance of Fintech Innovations and Blockchain

The technical revolution propelling the shift to T+1 is led by advancements in finance and blockchain:

Blockchain

Transparency and Security: While blockchain's security measures guard against fraud and illegal access, its transparency helps to build confidence among market participants.

Efficiency Gains: Blockchain technology dramatically accelerates the settlement process and reduces operating expenses by doing away with middlemen and the need for manual reconciliations.

Innovations in Fintech

Enhanced Risk Management: Fintech solutions with AI and machine learning capabilities offer real-time insights and sophisticated analytics, which enhance risk assessment and decision-making procedures.

Customer-Centric Solutions: Fintech companies provide cutting-edge products that improve user experience. By providing more accessible and efficient trading platforms, they may draw in a wider pool of investors.

Financing Systems for the Future

Financial institutions need to take deliberate measures in order to future-proof their systems and get ready for ongoing technological advancements:

Investing in Scalable Infrastructure

Modular Systems: Building modular and scalable IT infrastructure allows financial institutions to adapt quickly to new technologies and market demands without significant overhauls.

Cloud Computing: Leveraging cloud computing can provide the flexibility and scalability needed to handle increased transaction volumes and complex data processing requirements.

Continuous Learning and Development:

Training Programs: Implementing continuous training programs for staff ensures they stay updated with the latest technological advancements and best practices.

Collaborative Innovation: Partnering with fintech companies and participating in innovation hubs or regulatory sandboxes can foster a culture of continuous improvement and technological adoption.

Boosting Cybersecurity Procedures:

Sturdy Security Protocols: As financial systems get increasingly data-driven and networked, it is imperative to improve cybersecurity defenses against changing threats.

Frequent Audits and Assessments: Regular security audits and risk assessments help to find vulnerabilities and guarantee adherence to rules and industry standards.

Flexibility and Compliance with Regulations

Adapting to Regulatory Changes: For operations to run smoothly, it is critical to stay up to date on regulatory developments and make sure systems are adaptable enough to meet new requirements.

Proactive Engagement: Organizations can stay ahead of regulatory changes and have an impact on industry practices by proactively interacting with regulators to define future policies and standards.

The T+1 settlement cycle is made possible by technology, and real-time processing technologies, blockchain, and fintech innovations are at the vanguard of this revolution. To future-proof their operations and maintain their competitiveness in a market that is always changing, financial institutions need to invest in scalable, secure, and adaptable infrastructures. In order to make sure they are ready for the future of financial trading and settlement, institutions should embrace proactive regulatory engagement, collaborative learning, and ongoing learning.

Chapter 12

Responses and Adjustments from the Global Market

Regional Reactions and Approaches

Different financial markets have responded differently to the global switch to a T+1 settlement period. The adaptation approach employed by each location is a reflection of its distinct technology capabilities, legislative framework, and market dynamics. This chapter looks at how different markets have responded to T+1, noting both the difficulties and the successes encountered throughout the changeover.

North America: Taking the Lead
Americas

Proactive Transition: Encouraged by industry-wide cooperation and governmental mandates, the US has been a leader in the adoption of T+1. A seamless transition was made possible by the Securities and Exchange Commission's (SEC) clear standards and timetables.

Technological Investments: Major financial institutions made significant investments in technology advancements to make sure their systems could manage the higher volume and faster of transactions. Blockchain technology and artificial intelligence have been essential to this change.

Success Story: Better market liquidity and higher trade volumes accompanied the US market's 2024 shift to T+1. This triumph has established a standard for other areas contemplating analogous actions.

Mexico and Canada

Collaborative Approach: To align their settlement cycles, Mexico and Canada worked closely with the United States. By ensuring uniformity throughout North American marketplaces, our partnership decreased the risks associated with cross-border settlement.

Regulatory Support: Both nations' regulatory agencies offered robust assistance, collaborating with financial institutions to tackle technical and operational obstacles.

Europe: Progressive Adjustment
United Kingdom

Government Approval: In order to remain competitive in the global market, the UK government's approval of T+1 showed a clear policy requirement. The creation of a transition plan was greatly aided by the Accelerated Settlement Task Force.

Industry Readiness: Because EquiLend and other companies already have T+0 operations in the securities finance space, they have demonstrated readiness. By

2027, the UK market is anticipated to have fully implemented T+1, giving plenty of time for adaption.

Difficulties: Making sure smaller institutions can keep up with the required operational and technological improvements has been one of the main problems.

Union européenne

Diverse Responses: The European Securities and Markets Authority (ESMA) had a variety of responses to its T+1 Call for Evidence. While some market participants voiced concerns about costs and operational readiness, others emphasized possible benefits.

effect Assessment: In order to strike a balance between the advantages of quicker settlement cycles and the preparedness of its varied markets, the EU is carrying out extensive effect evaluations. Amongst member states, coordination is still a major obstacle.

Asia-Pacific: Diverse Advancements
Japan

Deliberate Planning: Prior to committing to a transition, Japan studied the effects of T+1 in other markets in a cautious but deliberate manner. The Tokyo Stock Exchange is now investigating ways to improve technology in order to facilitate quicker settlements.

Market Readiness: To make sure they can fulfill the needs of a shorter settlement cycle when adopted,

101

Japanese financial institutions are investing in cutting-edge technology like blockchain and artificial intelligence.

Australia

Regulatory Initiatives In assessing the viability of T+1, the Australian Securities and Investments Commission (ASIC) has taken the initiative. Preserving investor trust and guaranteeing market stability are the major priorities.

Industry Cooperation: Australia's approach relies heavily on cooperation between market players and regulatory agencies. Possible transition paths are being paved with the assistance of pilot initiatives and industry consultations.

Achievements and Difficulties

Success Narratives:

US Market Efficiency: The US is a shining example of a country that successfully adapted to T+1. The market demonstrated the advantages of a proactive and well-supported shift by experiencing higher liquidity, less settlement risks, and operational efficiencies.

North America in collaboration: The concerted efforts of the United States, Canada, and Mexico serve as an excellent example of the benefits of regional cooperation. Cross-border settlement cycle alignment has improved market stability and streamlined operations.

Problems:

Technological Barriers: Adapting their systems to meet the expectations of T+1 is a major barrier for smaller financial institutions across diverse areas. Technological improvements might be prohibitively expensive and difficult.

Regulatory Coordination: It is still difficult to provide uniform regulatory frameworks among various jurisdictions, especially in areas like the EU where several member states have to harmonize their laws and regulations.

Operational Workflow Modifications: Adopting T+1 necessitates significant modifications to operational procedures. To guarantee smooth execution and settlement, market players must modify their transaction matching, reconciliation, and liquidity management procedures.

The worldwide market has responded to the T+1 settlement cycle in a variety of ways, with each region implementing tactics that are specific to its own conditions. Although North American success stories serve as a model for others, operational, regulatory, and technological obstacles underscore the intricacies of such a momentous shift. As more markets transition to T+1, overcoming these obstacles and reaping the full rewards of a shorter settlement cycle will require ongoing cooperation, investment, and innovation.

Chapter 13

Wrap-Up

A Synopsis of the Transfer to T+1

An important turning point in the development of trading and settlement procedures has been reached by the global financial market's transition to a T+1 settlement cycle. This chapter provides a thorough review of the shift, its repercussions, and future possibilities by summarizing the main ideas and lessons from the previous chapters.

Important Notes and Learnings

Global Momentum: The transition to T+1 has gathered tremendous momentum globally, with North America at the forefront and Europe and the Asia-Pacific area following suit. The widespread advantages of shorter settlement times, including as lower counterparty risk, more market liquidity, and increased operational effectiveness, are highlighted by this global momentum.

Technological Advancements: The shift to T+1 has been made possible by important technological enablers like blockchain, artificial intelligence, machine learning, and real-time gross settlement systems. These technologies open the door for upcoming advancements in the financial markets in addition to facilitating quicker and more secure transactions.

Regulatory Support and Cooperation: The effective implementation of T+1 has been made possible by robust regulatory frameworks and cooperative efforts among market players. Regulatory agencies across many areas have been essential in establishing precise protocols, deadlines, and guaranteeing market preparedness.

Operational Adjustments: Process alterations, technology advancements, and improved risk management techniques are just a few of the major operational changes that financial institutions have had to make. In order to guarantee smooth market operations and satisfy the requirements of a shorter settlement period, certain modifications are required.

Economic Implications: There have been a number of advantages and difficulties associated with the switch to T+1. Higher trade volumes, lower costs, and improved market efficiency are all significant benefits of the shift, but it also comes with significant infrastructure and technology investments, as well as the requirement for efficient liquidity management.

Prospects for the Future: Moving to T+1 is a first step toward much more sophisticated settlement cycles. The banking sector may witness additional decreases in settlement times as technology advances, possibly leading to real-time settlements. Reaching these upcoming benchmarks will need constant innovation and adaptation.

Concluding Remarks Regarding Settlement Cycles' Future

Thanks to ongoing efforts to reduce risk and increase efficiency, together with technological improvements, settlement cycles are expected to continue improving in the future. The shift to T+1 is a component of the larger development of financial markets, not its conclusion. Real-time settlements (T+0)—transactions that are conducted and resolved instantly—may become more prevalent in the sector as fintech advances, blockchain technology, and artificial intelligence advance.

Real-time settlements have the potential to significantly reduce counterparty risk, improve liquidity, and stabilize the market. But reaching T+0 will need substantial technological breakthroughs, strong legal systems, and thorough market preparation. To stay ahead in this fast-paced environment, financial institutions need to maintain their agility, make constant investments in technology advancements, and promote an innovative culture.

To sum up, the switch to T+1 is a big step forward for the world's financial markets. Through the use of new technology, increased regulatory backing, and modifications to operational procedures, the industry is making great strides in achieving the full benefits of quicker and more effective settlement cycles. The path towards T+1 has created a solid base for subsequent developments, paving the way for a more robust, liquid, and effective global financial system.

Addenda
Appendix A: Terminology Glossary

Blockchain: A distributed, decentralized digital ledger that keeps track of transactions across numerous computers in a way that prevents transactions from being changed after the fact.

Counterparty Risk: The possibility that one of the parties to a financial transaction may not fulfill its end of the bargain.

Real-Time Gross Settlement (RTGS): A system in which securities or money are transferred individually and instantly without a credit or debit being balanced out.

Settlement Cycle: The time frame that starts on the day of the transaction and ends on the day it is settled.

T+0: On the transaction date, the trade is settled by same-day settlement.

T+1: Next-day settlement, in which the deal is finalized one working day following the date of the transaction.

T+2: Two business days following the transaction date, settlement is made.

T+3: Settlement occurs three business days following the date of the transaction.

Appendix B: T+1 Implementation Timeline
2021: The viability of switching to T+1 will be the subject of preliminary talks and industry engagements.

2022: Plans to switch to T+1 are announced by regulatory authorities in the US, Canada, and Mexico.

The UK government establishes the Accelerated Settlement Task Force in December 2022.
The EU's Call for Evidence on reducing the settlement cycle is released by ESMA in March 2023.

Andrew Douglas is named chair of the Technical Group in the United Kingdom in April 2024.

T+1 will formally go into effect in the US, Canada, and Mexico on May 27 and 28, 2024.

2025: T+1 operations in the UK will be subject to mandated adjustments.

The target year for the UK's T+1 implementation is 2027.

Technical Group Members and Their Roles, Appendix C

Douglas Andrew

Position: Technical Group Chair

Bio: Douglas has over 35 years of post-trade expertise and has held a number of senior positions in the financial services industry, specializing on settlement procedures and market infrastructure.

Gabi Mantle:

Position: EquiLend's Head of Post-Trade Solutions

Biography: Mantle is in charge of EquiLend's post-trade solutions, making sure that clients' systems and procedures comply with legal obligations as well as industry best practices.

Charlie Geffen

Advisor to the Technical Group is the role

Biography: A seasoned veteran of the financial sector, Geffen has a wealth of knowledge regarding the legal and regulatory facets of the financial markets.

Appendix D: Supplementary Materials

"Blockchain Revolution" by Don and Alex Tapscott: Don and Alex Tapscott's "Blockchain Revolution" is a thorough manual for comprehending blockchain technology and its possible effects on financial markets.

"The Handbook of Post-Trade Processing" by Peter Norman: Peter Norman's "The Handbook of Post-Trade Processing" provides a thorough examination of post-trade procedures and the difficulties associated with market settlement on a worldwide scale.

ESMA's Call for Evidence Reports: Detailed comments and analysis on the consequences of shortened EU settlement cycles are provided in ESMA's Call for Evidence Reports.

White papers from EquiLend: perspectives and research on securities financing and the shift to T+1.

Guidelines for the US transition to T+1: Best practices and guidelines from the Securities Industry and Financial Markets Association (SIFMA).

www.ingramcontent.com/pod-product-compliance
Lightning Source LLC
Chambersburg PA
CBHW050113230526
45470CB00004B/1810